Of Wings and Dirt

Of Wings and Dirt

A Collection of Poems

KIMBERLY PHINNEY

Foreword by Nicholas Trandahl

RESOURCE *Publications* • Eugene, Oregon

OF WINGS AND DIRT
A Collection of Poems

Copyright © 2024 Kimberly Phinney. All rights reserved. Except for brief quotations in critical publications or reviews, no part of this book may be reproduced in any manner without prior written permission from the publisher. Write: Permissions, Wipf and Stock Publishers, 199 W. 8th Ave., Suite 3, Eugene, OR 97401.

Resource Publications
An Imprint of Wipf and Stock Publishers
199 W. 8th Ave., Suite 3
Eugene, OR 97401

www.wipfandstock.com

PAPERBACK ISBN: 979-8-3852-1115-9
HARDCOVER ISBN: 979-8-3852-1116-6
EBOOK ISBN: 979-8-3852-1117-3

VERSION NUMBER 05/22/24

Scripture taken from the New King James Version®. Copyright © 1982 by Thomas Nelson. Used by permission. All rights reserved.

For my beloved husband and daughter.
For my God, my mother, and my person, C.W.

We are all miracles—made of wings and dirt.

When you pass through the waters, I will be with you;
And through the rivers, they shall not overflow you.
When you walk through the fire, you shall not be burned,
Nor shall the flame scorch you. For I am the LORD your God,
The Holy One of Israel, your Savior.

—Isaiah 43:2–3

To console those who mourn. . .
To give them beauty for ashes, The oil of joy for mourning,
The garment of praise for the spirit of heaviness;
That they may be called trees of righteousness,
The planting of the Lord, that He may be glorified.

—Isaiah 61:3

CONTENTS

Foreword by Nicholas Trandahl | ix
Acknowledgments | xvii
Preface: Deep Waters | xxiii

Dirt

A Brutal Love | 3
The Sculptor | 5
Angels Like Jazz | 8
Body of Work | 11
Here | 13
After the Rains in Hiawassee | 15
Garden Vespers | 19
Hunger | 22
Ache | 24
Haikus for Morning | 26
Mockingbird | 26
Gardenias | 26
Roots | 26
We All Do Fade as Leaves | 27
Multitudes | 29
Rivers | 31
Husbandry | 33

Woman

The Woman Speaks of Sequoias | 37
We Are Not Quiet | 38
A Mercy | 42
Daughter | 43
Haikus for Hadley | 44
Mother Love | 46
Witness | 47
A Conversation | 48
Out of the Mouth of Babes | 49
Women's Work | 51

Wounded

My Blue Octopus | 55
The Words | 59
Fire | 61
This Light Between Us | 62
On Lake Jocassee | 64
Bath | 67
Afterlight | 69
A Blinking Glow | 70
Firelight | 72
Aftermath | 74
Long Shadows | 76
Paper Doll | 79
Burn | 81
This Line, Residing | 83
Haikus for Mourning | 85
Old Friend | 85
A Home Once | 85
Self Portrait | 85
Blue Ridge Sky | 86
A Burning Observed | 87
This Dark-Fire Wonder | 90
Monochrome | 91

Wonder

A Series of Wonders | 97
Sacred-Making | 100
Air and Sound | 102
House Plants | 103
On First Reading Mary Oliver
   at The Sourwood Inn | 104
On Finding a Shovel
   Abandoned
   Mid-Work | 106
A Disturbance | 108
Cathedrals | 110
This Is My Happy Poem | 112
Haikus for Healing | 114
Heart | 114
Mind | 114
Soul | 114
Always | 115
My Monkish Life | 117
Awestruck | 120

Wings

Man of Sorrows | 125
This Holy Breaking | 127
Entertaining Angels | 129
Still Life | 132
Speechless | 134
A Liturgy for Suffering | 136
On Psalm 84 | 138
The Arrival | 139
Earthbound | 140
That We May See Its
   Goodness | 142
I'd Like to Believe | 143
This Holy Act | 144
There Is a Door | 146
Of Wings and Dirt | 148

FOREWORD

Nicholas Trandahl

I am a seeker of many things. Truth. Contentment. Pleasure. Nourishment. Community. In the luminous poetry of my friend Kimberly Phinney, I have found a sanctuary where I can settle in amongst all these things. As the poetry editor for a literary journal with a focus on mindfulness, spirituality, and nature, I have had the pleasure of reading and publishing some truly exceptional and likeminded poets. Most of the time, however, my work as a poetry editor begins and ends with the submittal process, where I go my separate way from the many poets I encounter after publication or rejection. There are a few special poets, though, who have graced me with authentic friendships following the transactional engagement of publishing. Kimberly Phinney is one of these poets.

When Kimberly submitted her poem "Body of Work" to the journal I work for, I knew instantly I was going to accept it for publication. That poem's lines pleaded for a reformation of the good sacred connections we have lost as a society with our world, both in a spiritual and physical sense. When I read them again and again, I knew they were written by a kindred spirit.

Kimberly is a relatively new voice in poetry, as a lifelong academic who poured her talents into her students. But she is a voice desperately needed in times like these. A world separates us physically: myself in the Wyoming high country of the northern American West and she in the humid eternal greenery of the American Southeast. But Kimberly has become a poetic sibling in a way. Our paths, though vastly different at first look, are actually quite similar.

With my journey as a military veteran struggling in ascent out of darkness and her long quest to rise out of the pain, loss, and confusion of chronic illness, we both have walked the agonizing trail of trying to heal—to grow out of the morass of suffering like lotus blossoms. And Kimberly's poetry is thick with that story—that path. Her readers heal with her; we kneel with her in devotion to her ardent faith.

I suppose it is so easy to accompany Kimberly because she is a leader, a community-builder. A devoted educator, she has also grown a community of faithful creatives as the founder and editor-in-chief of *The Way Back to Ourselves*, a literary journal and radiant resource for Christian creatives, as well as seekers of all paths reaching blindly for goodness and sacredness in our vicious 21st century darkness. A beacon or lighthouse in these storms of divisiveness and disconnectedness, *The Way Back to Ourselves* is as much of a guiding light as Kimberly herself.

Her debut poetry collection *Of Wings and Dirt* also serves as a guide through suffering, along the trails and simple miracles of being our imperfect selves, and finally into what it means to heal and grow. *Of Wings and Dirt* feels like a breviary to me, each poem a prayer of gratitude and authenticity. There is no posturing here in these poems you're about to read, just as there is no posturing in Kimberly herself.

I'll end these lines with a poem I wrote for Kimberly. I was a guest on her podcast, *The Way Back Podcast*, and in gratitude she mailed me a book of poems and new rosary, knowing I typically take a rosary with me when I go backpacking out in the wilderness. This was just prior to a very important surgery she needed to undergo.

So, on a cold autumn day, I found myself on the high limestone rim of a canyon in some burned-over wild country. It was a place of charred ruins, though over the years new vibrant growth had been coming back thicker and thicker. It was a landscape being rejuvenated by healing. So, of course, I thought of Kimberly, sat down on a boulder on the edge of the cliff, pulled out the simple wooden rosary she'd sent me, and I prayed a rosary for her. The rough draft of this poem "Rosary" came like a flood soon after.

Just days later, I was overjoyed to hear Kimberly's surgery was a miraculous success.

ROSARY

with gratitude to Kimberly Phinney

       Clicking
   along
the wooden beads
    of my rosary,

       following
   this strand
of prayers
       like a creek,
          luminous
   with autumn light,
     dense
with rainbow trout
       and thirsty muzzles
   of whitetail,
     elk,
and bighorn sheep,

    following
prayers
    where they lead,
       a trail

```
        climbing
            arduous
    seven-hundred feet
        to the limestone rim
            of the canyon,
        blue sky
yawning
        above,
            hawk
                carving
        sacred symbolism
in crisp clear air,


        me
        perched here
            at the edge,
        a holy fool
            or wild thing,
                unafraid,
            whispering
        words
repetitive,
            zen-like
        in the stained-glass state
of acceptance,
            anger
and sin
        flaking
from weary shoulders,
        a sweaty brow,
```

    breathing,

   breathing,

accepting,

     releasing
   like leaves
from trees
   crowded silent
      in icy shadows
   of the canyon floor,
golden yellow,
   orange,
     bright red
        given way
to late autumn notes
   of umber,
     burgundy,
       grey,
   letting go
of their leaves
    to rot
      among
   stones,
  bones,
and shattered deadfall,
    chipmunks
   and red squirrels
scampering,

              following
          those prayers
all the way
          to the understanding
               that all of this
          is the true prayer,
               never-ending,
          like love,
like how matter
               grows,
                    thrives,
          decays,
changes form
     and continues on,
               transforms
          endlessly
     into new life,
new forms,
     each one
so sacred,
          so beautiful,
               so holy
     that it's almost
               overwhelming,
          and I finish here
     though I don't want to
finish
     clicking
          through these prayers
               like mantras
     between thumb

and finger
            as the late patina
        of this day
    forces me
out of this graceful loop,
            this strand
        of cycles,
    like rebirth,
like beginning
    again
            and again
despite the fear
        and sorrow,
    the unbelievable heartache,
            the doubt
        that I'm enough
    or ever will be
            enough,
despite everything,

            standing
        ceaselessly
    to walk out
into vast primal spaces
    where the fire
            still burns
        within me,
where I know
    I'm also a part
        of the prayer,
    porous,

all sorts of miracles
>   filtered
>   through my substance,
flowing down,
>   connecting
>   endlessly
>   to everything else,
swept along
>   to places
>   I was never
>   prepared to go
>   but did anyway,
>   where I learn
>   how to be
>   a better man,
where I learn
>   how to love
>   more deeply,
how to be brave
>   and grateful,

>   clicking
>   along
>   the wooden beads
of my rosary.

ACKNOWLEDGMENTS

Writing and creativity are in my blood. I come from a long line of women writers and creatives. Both my grandmothers were gifted wordsmiths. In fact, one earned entry to the women's Harvard (named Radcliffe at the time) but missed her chance after a family tragedy claimed her father's life. Instead, she chose the nobler thing and stayed home to care for her younger siblings and grieving mother. My other grandmother earned three degrees when most women had none and went on to teach and write top-secret documents for the United States Government. My great aunt was Eleanor Boylan, mystery writer of the Clara Gamadge series, which earned her finalist status for the Agatha Award, named after Agatha Christie. She was a great inspiration in my young life. I still remember her typewriter in the hazy light of her bedroom and the aroma of old books and stout coffee. Eleanor's aunt, Elizabeth Daly, was the award-winning writer of the Henry Gamadge books—and she just so happened to be Agatha Christie's favorite mystery writer, too. My great aunt, several generations removed, was Betsy Ross, the woman who is remembered best in our history books as the seamstress who designed and sewed the first American flag under George Washington's request.

This rich history of strong women creatives beats hard in my chest, and I must acknowledge them first because they are a part of me. But long before I knew and understood any of this, I was writing. My first memories of the "writing fever" came to me when I was just eight years old. I wrote a mythical story of a little girl who found and tamed a cheetah that was living in the woods behind her home. Of course, that little girl was me. It seems I wanted to tame wild things since the beginning, which is of no surprise.

Then, in my early teens, the poetry came. I filled volumes of journals and notebooks with verse. So much so, that my mother found great frustration in the ineffectiveness of grounding me to my room for sassing or being too wild. She laughs and tells anyone who will listen, "I couldn't punish her! If I sent her to her room, it was a good thing. She'd just read and write!" We joke now that all the time I spent in my room being grounded is what contributed to my writing life today. I must thank my mother, not just for keeping my life full of books and blank pages to fill, but for denying me television. If I was bored, it was a "personal problem." I was always made to go outside, to run, to play, to read, and to think creatively. Ever the educator, my mother even played a guiding role in helping me write "The Sculptor," which is a poem that appears in this book and won runner-up in a small collection I submitted to a major poetry contest in 2023 with *Fathom Magazine*.

And, here, I finally arrive in my most present history: the life I live with my husband and daughter. I am forever grateful to God for giving me these two beautiful souls. We are miracles. My husband, as I have so often said, is my rock. He is my first and forever reader and, as he likes to say, my "most devoted patron." Whatever I have dreamed, he has been there to say, "Go for it!" If I have a vision, he is always there to help me execute it. He sees me for who I am and has carried our family through the darkest days, months, and years of my illness. If it wasn't for him, I wouldn't be here. And I certainly wouldn't be writing. We fell in love when we were just kids, and here we are. And of course, there is our dearest Hadley Rose—my old soul of a child. She has been my constant muse and central point of gratitude since the day she was born. I am better in every way because she exists. I thank her for giving me so many wonderous things to write and do in this world. No doubt, everything is more beautiful because she is here.

I am eternally grateful for my person and best friend, Candice Wolff, who told me in college that I was enough, that I would write and publish, and that God sent us each other—like sisters—to go through this life together. She also told me "Brave isn't a feeling; it's a doing." She was right on all accounts (as she often is), and her faith and unconditional love helped to propel me forward in the most hopeless of situations. She has stood by me for nearly half my life, and I know we will still be standing for forty more.

I am also specifically thankful for Anna Khoury, a former English student of mine, who cared for me during my illness and knew I "could write." It was Anna who encouraged me to write and submit to *Calla Press* after the most severe days of my illness. She saw something I couldn't. I listened to her, and several months later, my poem "A Brutal Love," which opens this very collection, was published in *Calla Press*. This is a full circle moment, and I am reminded again just how much God loves circles. I have that similar gratitude for Mr. Michael Dyck, who was an angel placed in my life when I was at my lowest point. He was my long-term substitute for my courses when I was ill at home. He is a godly man and father figure who cared for my students and me when we desperately needed his encouragement and protection. When I was losing everything—my job, support, classroom, and community—he told me he saw much greater things at play. He told me I might lose my classroom and the walls of room 925, but that God was about to give me a larger classroom without walls where I would impact many more souls for the Kingdom. Although it was an exceptionally kind thing to say, I didn't believe him—I was that broken and damaged. But he was right, and here I am. Again, I count the circles, and I see God's beautiful, firm hand drawing them all.

Saying "thank you" often isn't enough for certain gifts in life, like when people come to be your caretakers and prayer warriors when you are sick and have nothing to give in return. I am forever grateful to a collection of beautiful souls who came along to care for me and my family in a variety of ways during my prolonged illness: my family members and in-laws, my church family, the Wolff family, the Bullian family, Anna Eicholtz, Christina Reiss, the Willeke family, the Resa family, the Dyck family, Jan and Dan Bobik, the Ferry family, the Allen family, Amy Dayton, Susan Burton and the Prayer Warriors, the Crumley family, the Stefanic family, many of my beloved students, and so many others I wish I could name here.

I also must offer my deepest gratitude and acknowledgements to my faithful writing community and platform, www.TheWayBack2Ourselves.com, as well as all the editors, mentors, journals, news outlets, organizations, magazines, podcasters, and publishers who found merit in my work and nurtured both my talents and soul. Here is a small collection of many: the good people at Wipf & Stock, Good Morning America and ABC Action News, NSHSS, Conor Sweetman of *Ekstasis Magazine*, Stephen Roach of *Makers and Mystics*, Samantha Cabrera of *Calla Press*, Daniel Eccles of *The Opportunity Collective*, Troy McLaughlin of *This Undivided Life Podcast*, Deidre Braley of *The Second Cup*, Merrit Onsa of *Devoted Dreamers Podcast*, the editors at *Fathom Magazine*, and many more.

I also want to thank my editors and contributors at *The Way Back to Ourselves*: Sarah Steele, Ashley Whittemore, Kimberly Kralovic, Nicholas Trandahl, Steve Veasey, Matthew Nash, Zaher Alajlani, and Bethany Peck. They all came into my life when I needed community and friendship most. And of course, again, I must say thank you to Nicholas Trandahl for his stunning foreword, kind endorsement, and brotherly mentorship. For the gorgeous cover art that is exactly what I dreamed of in my head, I must (again) applaud the incomparable Steve Veasey, who is an authentic friend and creative. And for being guides and kind friends to me, I must thank Tanner Olson and Jodi H. Grubbs for their beautiful, heart-felt endorsements and support. I often feel like a pauper sitting at a banquet table of kings and queens. These people live that large in my head because of the love and support they have poured out.

And of course, and most importantly, I must lift my eyes unto the hills and thank my Maker and good Father for saving me once as a child into your loving arms and then saving me again through this horrific illness so that I might have bonus days on this Earth to beautify the Kingdom and show others your love, truth, and grace. I am your child, and you have never let me go. I pray, when my days are done, I may hear that most beloved phrase of all: "Well done, my good and faithful servant."

I know there are so many others who I have not named here to sing praise over. I thank you all, truly. Please forgive this poor poet's memory lapse and space limit. And to my readers, as well, you are all prayed for and loved. Always know that you belong here. May the following pages fill your hearts and souls with hope, wonder, and faith.

PREVIOUSLY PUBLISHED WORK

Calla Press: A Blinking Glow, A Brutal Love, Earthbound, On Psalm 84, Speechless, The Woman Speaks of Sequoias

Ekstasis Magazine: Afterlight, My Blue Octopus, Sacred-Making, That We May See Its Goodness

Fallow House: House Plants

Fathom Magazine: Cover feature: Angels Like Jazz; Runner-up Collection "Of Wings & Dirt" in Summer Poetry Contest 2023: Rivers, The Sculptor, This Light Between Us; My Monkish Life

Heart of Flesh: Bath, Still Life

Humana Obscura: Hunger

Radix: Cathedrals

Sunday Mornings at the River: Burn, On Lake Jocassee, We Are Not Quiet

The Agape Review: This Holy Breaking, Here

The Amethyst Review: We All Do Fade as Leaves

The Clayjar Review: The Arrival

The Dewdrop: Body of Work

The Reformed Journal: There is a Door

The Write Launch: A Burning Observed, Ache

Vessels of Light: A Conversation, Fire, The Words

Wild Roof Journal: Aftermath

PREFACE: DEEP WATERS

Dearest Reader,

The autobiographical pages before you are here because of a miracle. You see, God delivered me from critical illness in 2021, and many of the words that follow carried me out of a deep depression where I battled loss of the most extreme kind.

In a span of several years, I endured aggressive Stage 4 Endometriosis, had four life-restoring surgeries, was hospitalized for sepsis two times, lost my ability to have more children, lost my ability to walk, and lost my job, friends, and much of my community. It was in my battle to find the will to live, to learn to walk again, and to see God in the dark night of my soul, that these lines flowed out of me like pent-up water from a cracked pipe.

After the pipe broke and the words flowed with force, there was more and more brokenness to bring to my Father. So, there's nothing these poems don't explore: the miracle of motherhood after a decade of infertility, mental illness and physical trauma, personal failures and relationship struggles, shattered dreams and abandonment, and suffering and loss of all kinds.

But most importantly, the great undercurrent of this verse is the beauty of a Creator who absolves all our suffering and the deep wonder that is found when we learn to live despite our suffering.

I am not trying to be holy or present the Christian life in a tidy package. I am simply a bloodied saint—made of wings and dirt—trying to cling to our faith with all I have in me because He promises me (and He promises you), "When you go through deep waters, I will be with you."

I have been in deep waters, my friend. And I nearly drowned. *But He is with us.*

You see, my story may be unique to me, but nothing here is unique to the human condition. I pray you find yourself here in these lines. I pray you find comfort and beauty—whether you are treading deep waters or ascending a mountain top.

I invite you into the small spaces of my soul. May you feel known. May you feel awe. But most importantly, may you find your soul a little lighter and life a little sweeter because we met here among these pages.

You belong here,
Kimberly

Dirt

*Then the Lord God formed man of dust from the ground,
and breathed into his nostrils the breath of life;
and man became a living being.*

—Genesis 2:7

*But now, O Lord,
You are our Father;
We are the clay, and You our potter;
And all we are the work of Your hand.*

—Isaiah 64:8

A BRUTAL LOVE

In my garden, mid-bloom,
I take the sheers
and cut them to their knuckles.
Breaking their necks,
the petals shed like blood
on the sodden earth.

I stand over them.

I am brutal
to the roses,
to the day lilies,
and daisies.
To the gardenias,
I am brutal
and unyielding—
their burnt offerings,
white ash,
like a death before me
in the dirt.

But I know better.

Oh, it is a Brutal Love
that birthed the universe,
demanded Isaac,
offered Job,
and required the Cross!
His is a Brutal Love:
ancient and unyielding,
perennial and unchanging.
Oh, it is a Brutal Love
that sheered me mid-bloom,
that allowed for winter days
of barren grief—
a dark night of the soul
like a death before me.

But He knew better.

In His garden
there is a severe mercy
in His pruning—
a Brutal Love falling down like rain.
And in His season
there is a humming from the earth:
a green bud unfurled.

And He is standing over me.

THE SCULPTOR

A marvel, she is—
both sacred and stone—
sitting in my garden bed.
Her gray-white edifice
an ebenezer,
ever reminding me
like Jacob,
Surely, God is in this place.

My Mother Mary—head bowed
and hands clasped
in eternal prayer—
you are silent yet emphatic,
passive yet exhorting
as you speak to me
from your repose:
You must be in gardens.
You must stay on your knees.

So, I must stop to know.

Oh, I study her!
My mind (ever-working)
goes backward:

You were flesh once
and chosen, too.
You carried divine blood
in your womb,
the heaviness of prophecy
in your chest—
a mother to your son
and a fellow mourner
at the cross.

And here you are
with me.

A stolid form
upon the sodden ground.
Cement among the living:
the crawling lantana,
the humming bees,
and the pink bacopa.

Once you were
but water and mud,
mere elements from the earth—
without meaning.
Yet the artist
(*somewhere in California,*
they told me)
put you together—
erected you from nothing
but a holy image in his mind.

And I ask you, Mary,
Is this what God does?

ANGELS LIKE JAZZ

after Billy Collins's "Questions About Angels"

Sometimes,
I wonder about angels, too.
I wonder, like you,
if they have pulled up a chair—
invisible and unannounced—
and I am entertaining them
with my coffee clouds
in the late morning sun—
unaware,
as it spills light
through the slits
in the east window.

Or if they open
their delicate hands—
to catch my tears
as they slough
off my jaw
when nobody sees
or believes
in my pain.
And if they like my poems
at all—or not.

I wonder about that, too.
Or if I am their *cup of tea*.
And might they like me best?
Or do they even like tea at all—
like the sweet vanilla rooibos
on my nightstand
I never finish?

And I wonder, like you,
what they might feel,
or if their wings are heavy,
and if they read my mail
when it comes.
And when I bend to tend
my garden,
I wonder if two little ones
are with me to witness
my tenderness
and soft wishes
for the lost generations
that fell out of me too soon.

And I hope angels like jazz
like I do,
particularly Billie Holiday,
and most definitely "Blue Moon."
So, I hope they don't ever feel
alone or lonely,
like I do,
which are two different things,
as you know.

They must not—
I think—
because I suspect
they have been the ones
to give comfort
with their soft breeze
across my arm
I mistook for the wind.
And that lovely presence
in the shadows
cast down
from the sweetbay
magnolia last May
I mistook for you?
I suspect those were angels, too—
dancing among us,
like old lovers at the piano bar
long after the music stops.

BODY OF WORK

She said flowers
made garden beds
with their bodies
and I wondered
what my body made
and
how I was using
the time
using my hands to haul
using my tongue to say
heaving my arms to hold
what?

and how we are flesh
and how we are soul

and yet we forget
how to grow
something gorgeous
and perennial
like lilies
like poppies
like pink thrift
in desolate places

throwing their backs into beauty
we forget

like something useful
like soil
like water
or the earthen jars
cracked and marred by their maker
caught up in the work
paying no mind to their use
we forget

have we fallen so far up
from the earth from which we came?
fallen so far
from ourselves
our Maker
we forget?

yes
we have fallen away
from this body of work
from the work of
our bodies
our souls

HERE

It is here, among the longleaf pines,
I meet my soul and cease
its painful longings.
It is here, I am known
and greeted by the earth
as it rises up each side of me—
blue spined and unfolding across the sky.

Here, is the poetry of life
God molded and stretched out in his hands—
made to lie down in painstaking beauty.
Here, I am taught and whispered to
and told things no man or book
could ever teach.

It is here, and only here, that I am understood,
by *this* land—
so grand and infinite—
living and breathing long before
my heart formed
and learned to beat beside it.

And where mankind grows most thin,
I can hear the rolling peaks and gold child ivy,

calling me and singing together
their wordless myths.
They tell me I am so small—
so ephemeral
—but *enough*
for them.

And they welcome me—
like clouds, like stars, like morning dew—
to come,
to stay,
to fade away,
and then
to disappear
within.

AFTER THE RAINS IN HIAWASSEE

I.

I saw a crippled sparrow
from the old world
in my garden once—
after the rains,
among the puddles
and empty flowerpots.
I watched and watched,
as she hunted and swayed.
I couldn't know what,
but there was something
she was searching for.

II.

Broken and searching,
I went like her, too—
after the rains in Hiawassee.
I went out into the valley hills,
caught between the mountains,
all a blue like my wending soul.

I went
to see the Queen Anne's Lace,
holding dewy drops
in her spindly fingers—
fed.

To witness the airy moth
in gentle flight,
flitter white
against the rolling mist—
free.

To see the Japanese beetles
folded
and copulating
in their alabaster buds—
alive.

To hear the wet land
sing in chorus,
every blade of grass
a hungry green—
erect.

And finally, to stare
the whitetail deer
in her dark eyes—
to lock a look
and *be seen.*

III.

It all tasted like life to me—
moving together,
never asking
the title of the song
or losing touch
with its tempo.

All never needing
to be named.
All never questioning—
only known.
All never searching—
only found.
All never asking permission
to act, to eat,
to love, to move.

IV.

So, I swayed
with their rhythms
in the sweet clover fields—
forgetting where I came from
or what I was looking for.
I pressed my ear to catch
the humming Earth's refrain.
And then I danced
like I had never danced before.

And when my soul was filled,

I heard a sparrow's cadence—
like the little one in my garden—
light across the sky
with her perfect opened wings—
singing *home.*

GARDEN VESPERS

I.

My God, my God:
Do you hear my prayers?
These midnight vespers
I am whispering?
In my soft hallelujahs—
gently mouthed
and cupped by tears
that drop from
my cheeks
and travel down
into the soil below
in these gardens
you know
too well?

II.

I wonder
if only the lilies hear me?
Or maybe just the lantana?
Because I can scarcely summon

anything more than,
*Though you slay me,
I will trust.*
And I still wonder,
though I can't pray it,
*When enough is
enough?*

*Forgive me, Father,
for I have sinned.*

III.

I sit under the moon
and swaying palms
as I listen for your voice,
but it's the night train's
aria going south—
a clear bell in the silent air,
singing over us.
And I don't know why,
but it makes me
remember what I read
so many years ago,
that if you sing
to your house plants,
you help them grow.

IV.

Then, I wonder,

in my doubt,
if my prayers might help us all—
the songs I'm singing
out to you, God,
and over the flora
before me—
without a choral response.

Though you slay me,
I will trust.

And if maybe
my tears will help, too,
as weary and broken
as they are,
to grow these garden things
to life
and to somehow
revive my faith again—
even in this silence.

HUNGER

That grainy taste
is in my mouth again.
They keep telling me
that nothing lasts
(as if it helps).
But still, I wonder
how there can be
meaning without forever.

I need
the blade of grass
to live on in its green goodness,
never to be bludgeoned,
    the lark to fly on
    across her infinite skies,
    never broken-winged or crestfallen,
        the infant to want his mother
        and never leave
        that fragile bird's cage of a body.

It feels like blasphemy
to watch the gardenia
in peak bloom
wither into a brown ghost,

  to watch the cupped water in my hands
  be carried off downstream
  and vanish into vapor,
    to watch young lovers shrivel
    and hunch down toward parting,
    like nothing happened at all.

Oh, it is a bitter taste:
to kiss the ground one last time—
or each other,
  to watch the horizon swallow the sun—
  and hunger,
    to blink our eyes closed—
    and welcome the coming dark.

ACHE

Stooping down,

    here,

I remember the honey blooms
on my grafted kalanchoe
and the bursting April storm clouds
that
    brought
        my
            garden
back:
so hard-fought,
setting the night greens on fire
with gold,
opening their mouths—
alive.

I praised those miracle, myriad heads of life!
I counted them with my eyes—
felt their fight.
Yet, there inched that
small,
    black,

        thick,
              spotted
                      thing
devouring.

And I marveled at him, too,
as he gobbled the
flaming,
    nascent
        buds,
left to right,
in his invisible tines—
this miraculous being
that would soon
close himself off to the world
and transform.

A tear broke across my cheek,
and that ancient ache came
to gnaw inside my chest,
speaking:

To sing the caterpillar's praises
is to wish my flower's end.
And to save my sweet kalanchoes
is to wish the caterpillar dead.

HAIKUS FOR MORNING

MOCKINGBIRD

Walking alone through
the morning spruce, I heard her
stories touch the sky.

GARDENIAS

My white gardenias
sing their fragrant notes at dawn—
calling me to life.

ROOTS

I saw the river
wash away the ground below.
But roots find a way.

WE ALL DO FADE AS LEAVES

after Isaiah 64:6

The prophet said,
We all do fade as leaves—
dissolve as snow.

And yet it's said,
Eternity
is sown inside us all:

Fine golden thread
and needle,
in and out our ribs—

a cage to hold
our beating hearts,
a life to call our own.

At once, a ceaseless thing—
again,
a halted stone:

The breath inside
our rising chests

is not our breath alone.

The prophet said,
We all do fade as leaves—
dissolve as snow.

At once, a constellation—
again,
a dying glow.

MULTITUDES

after Acts 5:14

Oh, how she peaked out—
a crimson kiss
against the evergreen folds.
A nascent bloom, greeting the world anew—
a drift rose with so much promise.
To be this flower among the many—
to be chosen.

So, how strange it must have been
amid all her newness to see
a rose just as she,
but limp and losing
his ruddy hue?

How can this be, she asked,
*that in our beauty
surely we will not live on forever?*

It seemed a cruel trick
by the Gardner's hands—
as painful as a crown of thorns,
indeed.

How is it that mid-bloom
we begin to lose
the very life we carry?

My child, you must not fret,
the old rose said.
For when we lose our bloom
is when new life begins.
One day soon,
you, too, will fall to the ground,
and give yourself up for
for the multitudes.

RIVERS

after Isaiah 43:19

Tell me,
when did our bodies
forget how to dance?
How to move and
how to play and take wild chances
like our children do in their bodies?
Like the hills rising up to meet them?
Like the air breathing life in their lungs?

Lungs like gulping largemouth bass
drinking in the rivers.
Rivers like living waters moving through the world—
falling down and baptizing us from the sky.
Sky like sprawling blue mountains—
laying across the horizons like bodies.

Bodies we have forgotten how to use:
to be caught up in rhythms,
to be alive in the work,
to be bent over the land—
plucking heirlooms up from the earth
to feed our singing mouths.

Mouths exalting on Sundays
and lulling our babes to sleep at night:
"*Tis so sweet to trust in Jesus,*"
in the heat of the dark,
in the bend of our arms—
holding our children
who have not yet forgotten
the rivers.

HUSBANDRY

Go, carve out a sacred space
in the ground of your garden
for your lament.
Drop in the seeds of grief
and water them with holy tears—
the ones that only God will know.

Then wait, you precious soul.
Like magic,
like clockwork,
green shoots will sprout up
when you least expect them,
singing their arrival song
to bless you in your toil,
heralding, "*I am here.*"

Smile and know
this new life comes to tell you
your pain was not for naught,
and to say, *"Tender Heart,*
I see you are tired now
from all this husbandry,
this suffering.
So, come, let us bloom,

*take up some room,
and learn to be new—
again."*

Woman

*Then the rib which the Lord God had taken from man
He made into a woman, and He brought her to the man.
And Adam said: "This is now bone of my bones
And flesh of my flesh; She shall be called Woman. . . ."*

—Genesis 2:22–23

*By faith Sarah herself also received strength to conceive seed,
and she bore a child when she was past the age,
because she judged Him faithful who had promised.*

—Hebrews 11:11

THE WOMAN SPEAKS OF SEQUOIAS

after Langston Hughes's "The Negro Speaks of Rivers"

I've known sequoias:
I've known sequoia trees so ancient and old that their underground cities
    of tangled roots span deeper and broader than the human kind.

My soul has grown deep like the sequoias.

I walked among them in my mind—ruddy and wide, a perennial green—
while the world slept and spun on without me.
I watched them stand in the fire, like Shadrach, and walk out untouched
    as everything blackened and crumbled around them—dust to dust.
I heard their fallen seeds crackle like hot embers on the forest floor—
oysters breaking open in vibrating life—a small pearl inside.
And I remembered what my teacher said when I was small:
"The great sequoia seeds need fire to regenerate—
burn them up, they break open, and come back to life."

Yes, I've known sequoias:
Phoenixes, burned by their Maker—
resurrected and set apart.

My soul has been burned like the sequoias.

WE ARE NOT QUIET

At first, we are quiet.
I am crouched over,
my cheek against my thigh.
My mother, too, is crouched
on the floor beside me
and tangled in my grip.
In spirit, we are kneeled
like twin saints
waiting
for the painful
Revelation.

I moan like some creature—
visceral
and wild—
as I am emptied out,
and everything runs into everything else:

old tree swings   running in the heather fields
    squealing in delight   and hiding beneath the blooming tangerines
listening to the whippoorwills   as they put the sun to sleep
    years on end
then walking across stages   and down aisles   hearing yes and I do
    and feeling solid for the first time in a long

                                        long
                                            while

My mother's face sings tears for me
but betrays her prophesies:
"There's still hope," she repeats,
but she is lying
to herself
(or is giving me
the mercy
of her lies—
offered up as small trinkets
on a tarnished plate).

She begs God out loud
to save this soul.
Again and again—
a chorus line on Sunday:
"Oh, Sweet Jesus!
Oh, Sweet Jesus!
Help us, if you will."

So, we bow our heads
and clasp our hands.
But everything runs into everything else:

his pale eyes spark and hold mine   his tenor on my chest
    longing   and feeling saved
hearing a plane in the sky and wondering could this be his
    and thinking   three   three   three
then the losing   and the cursing of that chromosomal flaw

and my broken body
like God did the devil   and listening to the voice in my head
*   screaming there is no knowing   anything*
but the giving and the taking
*   amen and amen*

It is strange how I am both—
alive and dead—
and how I twist to see
the red tendrils trail
in the water beneath me,
knowing there is nothing now,
but
waiting
for a Miracle
that
will
not
come.

There is silence again
before my hot grief escapes
in the yelp of an animal's pitch.
And it is loud
because I know
what my mother cannot admit
yet.

I flush and wonder where
your little soul goes:
Down the pipes or up to Heaven?
And it feels like a betrayal

in my head.
Or perhaps a tiny funeral instead.

We are kneeled like twin saints—
emptied and panting
in the Revelation—
when everything runs into everything else:

and from the living room I can hear   between our audible cries
    a clapping and a whooping
my father sounding his barbaric yawp   for his favorite team
    who has won the championship
and the world spins on   with you dead
    and we are not quiet for a long
                          long
                                  while

A MERCY

What if it's true?
What if this tiny angel took mercy on me?
Poked a hole in the clouds
to peer down?
Pulled back the black robe
between the stars
to hear my pleas flung up to Heaven—
again and again?
To witness all the times I cried
and spoke "Amen."
To witness all the times new life
became false starts
and broken hearts
we had to mourn.
Did she see it all?
And did she go to God
to say,
"Send me"?

DAUGHTER

And it was you
        with Billie Holiday on the record player.
And you
    with the blueberries diced and smeared on your face
                              I waited for.

And when the winter sun was slant at 45 degrees
                            bent across the glass
and setting fire to your tawny eyes,
                it was you.

You,
    my sweet one,
        you.

HAIKUS FOR HADLEY

I.

You are a meadow
of swaying heather, painting
Heaven lilac hues.

II.

You are a poem
little birds sing in the sky,
calling: Sun, awake!

III.

You are a flower,
using your body to make
beauty in gardens.

IV.

You are my prayer,
sung and cried one million times

into existence.

Amen.

MOTHER LOVE

On this early
morning waking,
I see.

This child:
born from
my broken body,
born to fill
my empty places,
to smooth
my jagged pieces,
to call me
to myself
and beyond
what I thought
I could be,
to know
and give
a sacred gift
made real
because of her.

WITNESS

The new spring sun spills
iridescence through
her pinwheel
on the sidewalk,
bathing it in blue
and purple hues.

And she says,
"Mommy,
look at God.
Do you see him
in the colors?"

I marvel
at my child-sage—
a Magi bearing gifts—
as I witness her
doing what children do:
finding God
where we
have missed.

A CONVERSATION

Child:
Mother, why do they hurt me so?

Mother:
Because you burn bright, my love.

Child:
And Mother, why does this world break our hearts?

Mother:
Because we have hearts that can stand breaking.

Child:
And why does a dove fall out of the sky?

Mother:
Because she was made for flying.
And nothing is made to last.

Child:
But Heaven?

Mother:
Yes, but Heaven.

OUT OF THE MOUTH OF BABES

Today, a little girl died from cancer
on the St. Jude's commercial.
I shed a tear, as I often do,
when my little girl stood up
and walked out of the room.

Silent moments—
pregnant with pause—
passed.
Then a pitter-patter of feet
came back
from down the hall.

"Mommy, that was so very sad,"
she whispered,
as she settled in beside me.
"I know, my love—
Are you okay?"
I asked, as I brushed
her blonde wisps from her face.
"Yes, Mommy. I can be—
somehow—
because I know she's in Heaven now. . .
And in Heaven, they say

there is no more pain—
no sickness—
and no disease."

New tears flowed down my cheeks.
"That's right, my love,"
was all I could say—
as I blessed God for Heaven
and this child's sweet belief.

We held a space there—
together—
for a moment in time,
as we spoke of love and faith
to process the heavy things
we face in this life.

And then,
like every child has done—
before and since—
she asked,
"Mommy, can I go play?"

WOMEN'S WORK

My little girl couldn't sleep tonight—
my gentle, anxious child.
And though my body hurt so much,
in that bone-aching way of exhaustion,
I summoned my strength
for this midnight shift
of motherhood
I dare not miss.

And I thought to myself,
deep into my watch—
These are the most important stories
I will ever tell.
These are the most important songs
I will ever sing.
These are the most important prayers
I will ever say.
This is the most important work
I will ever do.
To be here for this tender heart.
To bear witness to her needs.
And to tend to them with all myself.

So, let the dishes stack, I say.
Let the poems sit.
Let ambitions cease a while.
Tell the world to wait.

There's nowhere else I rather be
than to be right here with her—
doing *this* woman's work.

Wounded

Be merciful to me, O God, be merciful to me!
For my soul trusts in You;
And in the shadow of Your wings I will make my refuge,
Until these calamities have passed by.
—Psalm 57:1

And He said to her,
"Daughter, your faith has made you well.
Go in peace, and be healed of your affliction."
—Matthew 5:34

MY BLUE OCTOPUS

I.

In your cloud of arms,
pressing down,
I am dragged:

Oh, you invertebrate!
I am no match for your grip
(eight-fold and tentacled).
My Medusa, my Leviathan—
you blue-ringed,
bulging,
bulbous thing
I am unable
to shake
or swim
without.

II.

In your deep waters
I go
    down,

down,
    down:

Oh, how you collapse me—
flattened and unrecognizable—
like you,
soft-bodied and disappearing
into
the
smallest
of
spaces.

I am held close—
cradled and anesthetized—
like your prey,
an enveloped nervous system
in your electric glow.

Down,
    down,
        down
            I go.

III:

In your den, so familiar,
I am reminded
how to survive:

Oh, to ask the right questions

of death
and my despair.
Oh, my Blue Octopus!
Are you my predatory guide?
Pointing me eight-times
to watch the pearls fly
as they float to the surface—
those miniature pockets of life
I am meant
to trail behind?

Did I hear you mouth,
"Save yourself"
or was it
"Stay a little while"?

I do not know.

Or am I now a part of you?
A scrap of the living
you keep
in your cavern,
going on and on in
our own mythology—
and finally seeing
in our decay
and drowning
that under
great pressure,
we need only
bleed ink

to survive?

THE WORDS

There are winter words
I would use:
snow—plowed under;
troughs of icy encasements;
white banks
and heavy-laden slumber.

There are only winter words—
breaking off parts in frigid snaps
and draining greens to gray.
I know them all too well
and the silence
the barren land provokes.

Oh, I know the silence.

"It is never good," I tell myself,
when it settles in,
when the last rusty leaf falls
from its tree to kiss
the icy roots of snow,
and the writing stops again.

Then comes the prolonged winter:
a December without end.
The frigid breath comes to rest
in my bones and whispers that
the sun should set in its slant,
and the cold is welcomed in.

Oh, I know the silence.

The shivering and the pleading—
man against the wind.
The shivering, the pleading,
then the silence
once again.

But then.

The glacial peaks begin to crack and avalanche
by some deep work of God.
There's some small warmth at hand
underneath the ice,
and the break gives way to life.

Then spring words,
then summer words,
words flowing from the Stream.
The writing words—
familiar friends—
all come back to me.

FIRE

my mind:

i prefer its slow burn–
    its fireworks across a blue-black sky,

its tortuous brushfires
    to nearly anything else.

and though it burns me
    to the third degree,

it is—nonetheless–
        light.

THIS LIGHT BETWEEN US

I.

One night in late July, there was a look
right here on this lone mountain road—
lit with headlights where I watched
the doe's eyes catch and stare into mine
through the glass. And instead of
disappearing into the woods' dark mouth,
I remember her trembling
and suspended body before
our truck struck her, soft-footed
in a moment full of grace—
yet stunned in the light
beyond her instinct to survive.

II.

Then there was the satin moth's *hello*
that balmy night in August. I recall
writing by the light, with the old screen
cracked open to the black cloak of sky,
and how she came in, transfixed
by the magnetic, burning glow.

And I remember the gentle whisper
of her wings against the bulb,
and how I could not make her go.
So, I killed the light and slept.
And in the morning, there she lay,
dead on my bedroom floor.

III.

I have sat up,
and I have thought about these things
well into the early morning hours
when the world is still asleep.
And it is too much with me
to know—and not know—
who I am in the story,
or where to go
with this light
between us,
and what
it means:
the shining fires,
the soft dead bodies,
two worlds colliding—
yet never meant for
one another.

ON LAKE JOCASSEE

 I.

Horses drug us across the spine
of the mountainside,

  and I hardly heard the guide
  carry on about the specific

binominal nomenclature, plant species,
and hearsay of the region—

  I swatted flies from my face
  in the August heat

and worried about
my own depression

  pacing well behind the
  pack until he stopped us.

II.

Look here through those pines
and you'll see

the fabled Lake Jocassee,
he told us.

Legend calls it a great tragedy—
what happened

> to the Cherokee
> Princess.

So, I listened to him tell her story
and wept for her death.

III.

Sweet Cherokee Princess
of this blue native land,

> they say your name
> meant "place of the lost one,"

and I wonder if they knew
you'd live up to

> your call when you stepped off
> the ledge for love

and walked across the Whitewater River
toward that rival tribe to meet

    your dead Nagoochee
    whose ghost was waiting for you

like me.

BATH

Bleary eyes, sinews, joints,
all afloat
and submerged—
I wash away
the day's remains.

And I think:
I want to di(v)e.

I plunge a foot below
(a cross at 20,000 leagues)—
where spine and porcelain
touch
in forever pose.

I blink and gaze
through murky grays
and think how warm
this hazy nothingness
might be (without me).

And I hold my breath
until the burning fire
builds and buoys,

parting my bodies of water
(a little Red Sea).

I emerge and gasp
in this broken flesh He bought—
joints, sinews, and bleary eyes—
all bone-soaked
(and baptized).

And I think:
I want to live.

AFTERLIGHT

To sail into a thunderstorm is not so
commonplace: to have your body split in two,

to feel the electric fissures become you
and learn the cracks as you navigate

in your upside-down way.
Your pulsating heart, your pulsating brain—

both opened to calamity. Some might call
this chaos pain, but the good rain

poured in and flooded me.
And though I ached and rocked like those tiny

boats at sea, there were seeds planted deep
within me—hibiscus and white lily—

waiting for the tempest winds to break
and wake me from the dark

with His afterlight—
to bloom.

A BLINKING GLOW

with love for Candice Wolff

I'm still searching
for that something
inside of me
(or outside me)
where it has been promised
I will find a better self—
a Lighthouse.
Oh, that blinking glow in the dark,
roaring, ceaseless waves
where souls lost at sea
find higher ground—
a Rock.
That firm, cool terrain
where turbulence no longer
stalks the mariner,
where there are no more salty tears
or winged harbingers,
no dogged days
or endless dark.
But just a *mark*
on a map
where I can

stay a
little
while.

FIRELIGHT

after Luke 22:56

I had my chance, didn't I?
To say I knew you,
seated there in the firelight.
To whisper your good deeds
and tell your stories
and how you rescued me
from the edge.
To willingly risk
my life for yours
was not something
I was prepared to do
that night.
So, in my brokenness
I said, "No, no, no,
I do not know
this man you say I do."
How crestfallen
you must have been
because of my betrayal.
To be the God of the Universe
and denied a friend.
To be the Son of Man

and then abandoned
by nearly everyone
who claimed to love you.
What prophecy I had denied!
But you knew.
My God, my Friend,
forgive me
for I have forsaken you.

AFTERMATH

unthought of in any real way for what you were
propped up more so as my paper doll of vanity
I kept under glass
and a particular number
so many times you were in hell
you beautiful and starved thing
you were allowed to be violated and forgotten
even denied
oh I could not even stand to be with you alone
preferring the company of others
so many times you told me
what you needed
you insomniac
you neurotic
you crazy heat
I could not tame
so I gaslighted
I lied
I analyzed
your imperfections
then forgot you
until I needed you again
you warned me so many times
cried out

ached
and rebelled
but I did not listen
it is true
I only cared what others thought
and it was not until you bled broke and burned
and then threatened to die on that table
that I realized what I was doing
not until the doctor's cuts
endless pills
and tragedies we made
was I made to listen
and when I say all these things now
staring at you
touching you
oh they are dark judas-like betrayals
and I am sickened by how I treated you
my body

LONG SHADOWS

We are in the long shadows now—
stretching out
across the leaves of grass
in our suffering.
And we are losing light,

in the muted slivers I touch.

Her golden rays—

patterned and

oscillating distortions—

move across the land.

We beg her to stay,

keeping the hope

despite the fade.

And though we reach

and pray

the Sun answers not

but runs

after her horizon—

like doomed lovers do,

like Cleopatra after Mark,

like Tristan and Isolde.

So, the fade grows dark.

The air shifts cold.

The din of night descends

upon this hospital bed.

And we are left holding on

to what could have been.

PAPER DOLL

I take on shape again,
but still, I am a shattered
and burned up
version of myself:
an ashen heap—
a pulp pressed down
and cut and strung
together like those flimsy
paper dolls.

I am a two dimensional
burden now:
once known—
then a clouded face,
expressionless—
and at last,
forgotten waste
by those who claimed
to love me most.

But even so,
I smile for them
(or hide from them)
to cover up

my suffering.
But one by one,
they leave—
like ants in a line—
as everyone says,
"She'll be just fine!"
And some of them think,
"She must be lying. . ."

But only I know
the fire lit
inside me,
the staples and knives,
my broken insides,
standing on the edge,
talking with Death,
and the aftermath
that remains
long after
life moves on:
the paper,
the scissors,
scoring marks across the page
to pull forth a form,
to call it a girl,
and then to knock it down
with a single breath.

BURN

I know how to burn
    how to do it in secret
how to be doubted
    how to kiss death on his mouth
and be called a liar
    as if this fire inside me
did not grow wild
    did not consume me
and swallow my youth
    did not devour my generations
did not push me
    splayed on the surgeon's table
like cancer they said
    like an ashen heap
again again again and again
    like a wick lit at both ends
like hot filament inside the bulb
    like embers left to smolder alone
like broken glass
    or fissured cracks
like spider webs
    like gnarled roots
like roses dead
    thorns

    sickness
  blooming
     &n
bsp; membranes
    invisible
        oh I know how to burn

THIS LINE, RESIDING

The pain comes in the night
to bite at my insides:
a black wolf,
stalking in the woods,
juts out from between birch and pine—
fangs placed just right.

And I am reminded:
We are not so different.

This line, residing
between us,
is really just
one unexpected
disaster away
from being blotted out:
to be woman
or some wild thing.

Then, like clockwork—
the snow falls,
dawn licks at the horizon
with a beam of light—
the Sun—

and the predator backs
away into the dark
robe of trees.

And I am alone,
again,
in the quietude
of my relief:
still woman—
just barely.

HAIKUS FOR MOURNING

OLD FRIEND

I thought I heard you.
Her laugh was open like yours.
Sometimes, hearts play tricks.

A HOME ONCE

At what point does it
happen when the wind changes,
and you're carried off?

SELF PORTRAIT

I thought I knew you,
but we sometimes find strangers
looking in mirrors.

BLUE RIDGE SKY

Little mountains
in my mind
help me to be okay—
to find the will,
to stop the pain.

Here right now
is all we have—
is all I need:
to melt away
into Blue Ridge sky,
forgotten by all—
but *free*.

A BURNING OBSERVED

I had been dead
for almost too long—
that burning decay
made good on its
promise to
light a decrepit fire
through my veins,
to consume
health and light,
to force all good
to fall away.

On that bed,
a void of sorts,
I only had my mind—
and it turned to water:
flowing from pipes
and down drains,
dripping from childhood spickets,
then falling down like rain,
filling swimming pools,
then dancing in oceans,
all submerging me
like John did the Christ.

And I thought of
the Whitewater Falls
of the Carolinas
surging
and then standing
at its mountain ledge.
I felt a burning then, too,
as I watched the waters
converge
and rush out down
past the rocky summit—
overcoming debris and
defeating every pillow moss rock
that stood
before its power.

How I was swept up, too!

Like fire,
the waters devoured,
but it was better.
It brought life—
feeding the sourwoods
and famished blackberries,
beckoning the brown trout
upstream for spawning,
and filling its watcher
with a belief
in something
that was grand and new.

Oh, there is a reason why
my burning dreaming
turned to water:
Always, always, always—
water puts out fire!

THIS DARK-FIRE WONDER

If I walk backward
toe to heal
the back of my head
cutting the air
between now and then
my hair splitting in the wind
blowing back to cover
my face
my eyes
would it be different?
Would I?
Would you?
Can we get back?
Back to before broken?
Back before age
and illness and despair
became our bedmates
to smother our dreams
and our youth?
Because if I could
walk this dark-fire wonder back
back to the start
I would
I would
I would.

MONOCHROME

Do colors have meanings or feelings?
Do they make sounds or songs?
Do they come alive?

Because my world is dimmed
to a darkened light.

There is no music now.

In everything,
there is a draining—
a bleeding out
of color.

And at last,
a lament!

The reds have turned
to gray or brown,
as I drown in the fade,
like the winter does
to autumn leaves.

The trees birth colors
in one last
display of life
before they drop and shed.
Then all else turns to black or white.

There is no color now.

All else cold.
All else monochrome
for a long hard freeze
that works to kill.

Thin charcoal outlines
against stark sky.
Branches turned veins
like pathways in hands.
And those palms
reach out
to touch the stars.
Then Saturn.
Then Heaven,
asking for a reprieve.
To send the colors
and songs.

There is no hope now.

But underneath
the heavy banks of snow
there is a small trembling—

a hint of life:
a seed has dropped
where no one saw.
Now, a shoot beneath
the snow breathes
green.

A color.

The sound of laughter.

Then a bud.

And one fine morning——

the music starts.

Wonder

*Many, O Lord my God, are Your wonderful works
Which You have done;
And Your thoughts toward us
Cannot be recounted to You in order;
If I would declare and speak of them,
They are more than can be numbered.*

—Psalm 40:5

*For now we see in a mirror, dimly,
but then face to face.
Now I know in part,
but then I shall know just as I also am known.*

—1 Corinthians 13:12

A SERIES OF WONDERS

I.

Perhaps it is true
a whole Universe can be found
in the smallest detail:
unfolded in a bud opening in the sun,
called forth in an infant's laugh,
pulled down from the widow's cry.
But I wonder are they the same
to God?

II.

Do you ever wonder if
we are all going
backward to childhood—
to heal or relive something—
like vagabonds?

III.

And can I tell you I made a list of sad things?
An empty hot air balloon,

a full parking lot at the funeral home,
taking down the Christmas tree,
putting up fences,
realizing you were wrong,
realizing you were right,
unanswered prayers,
paper cuts,
lone trees,
mirages,
and
me.

IV.

One day, I realized I was so busy
counting shadows
I missed the sunset.
And I wondered how many ways
I had already died.
Do you know?

V.

And when did we stop carrying promises?
And start dealing in regrets?

VI.

I looked too long at a rainbow once—
after a torrential summer rain.
I was driving.
And I thought:

*Of course, I would die
looking at something beautiful.*

VII.

And don't you find it strange
we live
so long
we forget
everything?
Or we die
so young
we lose
everything?

VIII.

I wonder.
I do.

SACRED-MAKING

plucked from the vine my hands
wash you clean

red in bloom i waited for
you i cradled and read

you like fine-printed wonder black
and white on the page

like double suns on ocean
horizons halting man

to stare like a newborn's mouth
predawn crying for mother's milk

this divine quotidian act
we make as i cut you in halves

your twin chambers in twos pulse
your meaty valves breathe life

a fruit they say
a heart like mine

we beat together
in this sacred-making

i eat

AIR AND SOUND

We walked the empty mountain paths—
all dirt and barren trees.
And on the cold, clear air,
voices carried a joyous rapture—
calling in the new year.

And I thought of the mason jars
in the rustic cabin kitchen
that I wish I had
in my large jacket pockets,
so I could bottle the air and sound—
like fireflies—
and carry them with me
in the days and months ahead
that are named
healing.

HOUSE PLANTS

This fold of copse
I keep—
all evergreen
and at ease—
all leaves
of grass
and dirt—
know a thing
or two
about
the Light:
to find it,
to move toward it,
and to bow—
ever still
in its
presence.

ON FIRST READING MARY OLIVER AT THE SOURWOOD INN

I still think of the gnarled, rocking hands
of the old physician.
And his cataract eyes in a cloudy blue
like the mountains framed
in the paned
glass before us.
And the folded sliver of paper
(another kind of scalpel)
shaking before me.
Read, he said,
And enjoy your stay
at the Sourwood Inn.

With open windows,
swaying white sheers,
and my husband asleep
beside me,
I read the poem
to the wind and rain
of Asheville,
and I was changed:
a nudge, a gentle epiphany,
or a sprawling sense of knowing. . .

I do not know which cut
to my heart it was,
but I was captured
and held tight in the storm.

And yet
I cannot remember that poem—
its name, its words,
what it said, or where it went.
Since I have known her,
I have bought Mary,
read her and searched
for that poem again and again:
in gardens, in sickness,
in plenty, and in the mountains
of my mind—
just to find that sense of life.

I still do not know.
But perhaps
it was about dancing.

ON FINDING A SHOVEL ABANDONED MID-WORK

I came upon the pointed digger—
a spade facedown
in a mound of earth,
dusted in the rust of night
when the rain and dew came through—
all decorated in that fine silken thread,
the webbings of a delighted house spider
who made her home in the handle's cove,
whose hewn form had long-faded
to a driftwood gray
and now splintered under
the heat of day.

I stood and marveled
where its master
may have gone,
or what may have called
him away too soon
from his labor—
and then never
to return.
How many days
and nights
had come

and gone
since?
I could not tell.

And even now,
I am still left—
like that pointed digger—
to wonder.

A DISTURBANCE

I was five
    when I found the robin's eggs
    nestled in our spruce tree
    and touched them.

Awe-filled with disbelief,
    I held the oblong, blue bodies—
    like rounded sky—
    in my trembling hands.
Those smooth, speckled, electric shells
    with a silent galaxy inside—
    and a womb, too,
    cradling their hidden, downy souls.
So close to life and so young,
    I quivered—
    seeing their sacred wings in my mind's eye
    trace their future skies, like Heaven.

Oh, the magic of life
    that set my legs to running!
I called my mother to come see
    what God had done!
And when she came, I held them up,
    as she stood over me

and cried.

I thought
    she was crying because they were so beautiful.
I learned
    there are many ways to be wrong.

CATHEDRALS

We went out early
to water our tomato tree,
a ripening Park's Whopper
potted beside the yellow onions.

From the stalk to the ledge
there was something
birthed overnight:
all air shine,
fine-threaded and intricate
it stretched,
holding court
with drops of dew,
gleaming in the light.

"Oh!" I gasped,
as I marveled
at the spider's web.
How she must have
toiled in the dead
of night to produce
this holy silk:
so delicate, too,
and yet so indestructible.

Those tiny spires
and vaulted ceilings
patterned with her chisel,
all held tight at the center
and spun out hexagonal.

At once, I was gazing
at the Gothic turrets
of Notre Dame
before the fires
marred her.
At once, the flowers
in the foreground
became the spider's
stained-glass windows,
and I felt the urge to kneel
and kiss the ground
in prayer.

And I heard:
Who needs the trappings
of four walls
or to travel to the city,
when everywhere
in nature
there are cathedrals?

THIS IS MY HAPPY POEM

Our three flashlights in hand
all go out
when we arrive
for our "small adventure,"
as she calls it.
We need nothing but
the rock-salt moon
in full glow,
peppered by the clouds
in our midnight home.

Upside down perspectives
make us free and young
(again).
We pump our legs,
and our high-pitched shrieks
echo in a chorus of sound and stars
against our quiet town.

He pushes her.
Her fair ponytail bobs
against the black drapes of sky.
I am quiet
(and smile to myself)

as I move through the air.

We are swinging in the dark.
And I am alive.

HAIKUS FOR HEALING

HEART

Hand to heart and breathe.
Feel Him beat fresh blood through me.
I am new again.

MIND

Settle in silence.
Clear the mind to fill it with
Love. That's all there is.

SOUL

That invisible,
beautiful thing that runs through
you *is* you. Be awed.

ALWAYS

Poems are songs
set to the soul's rhythms,
naming the unknowns
with mirrors
held up to our hearts—
sweet psalms
knowing what we cannot.

And though there may
never be answers
for our questions Earthside,
as we grasp at this Holiness,
there will always be trains
singing in the key of G
through the night—
and always ears to hear.

And there will always be tea
somewhere at noon—
and always kindred to share.
And there will always be babes
crying out at dawn's light—
and always mothers to meet them.

In all the unknowing,
there will forever be
this call and response—
this give and take—
this ebb and flow.
And there will always,
always be
songs for souls—
this poetry.

MY MONKISH LIFE

I.

I fell asleep late last night
reading Isaiah
and dreamt about gardens
and prophecy.
I had nowhere I needed to be
when I woke,
so I slept in bed until noon,
listening to the rain hit the roof.
And when I opened my eyes,
I witnessed the humidity's dew
gather so gently
and drop down the windowpane
and cry tears like we do.

II.

Then, I watched my old pup awake
with my movements and rhythms
to do her faithful stretches—
a happy baby,
a downward dog.

And she reminded me
in her ease
that I should do more yoga
because they say
it's good for the pain.

III.

It's so quiet now.
I can hear the prayers in my head
and poetry lines run on and on.
So much so, I can't catch them all.
So, I think I may drink my coffee in bed
and learn to soak this silence in
some more, while my body rejects
the world and what it used to do.

IV.

And then I'll stop and write to you:
Listen, I think I can hear God overhead
because I finally understand
I am not a performance
or what others have said I am.
My worth is not measured by
what I am not producing here (in this bed).
It's almost as if my monkish life
is helping me to forget
all the broken parts in my past
and in my body
and those who have gone

because of it.
Time is good at making
hazy fragments
fog over like glass.
And God is good at healing.

V.

Yes, I think I'll drink my coffee in bed,
turn the clocks facedown,
read some Romans or Rumi or Rilke
out loud—
and keep relearning.
And maybe later
if I can get this ache in my belly to stop,
I'll go study the clouds
because for the first time in my life
I am living the art of "now."

AWESTRUCK

There are mysteries
I tremble to put down on the page.
Yet, I know they make
the very best kind of writing:
the unvarnished, eternal truth
about me,
about you,
about the world,
and the universe we spin on in,
and the quilt of stars
we'd find out there,
which they say
(whoever they are)
is multiplying as we speak
—or write.

Every work on the page
(or canvas)
that finds truth
is like a star.
It burns brightly.
And I am working hard
to multiply them
with my humble hand:

like Michelangelo did the David
and the Sistine Chapel,
like Vivaldi did with his Spring
in Four Seasons,
like Victor Hugo did
with his word-cladded cathedrals,
or like Saint Teresa of Avila
with every orphan she loved and fed.
All saints uncovering the mysteries,
reaching for God,
and finding Him.

And then,
like God did
and does forever—
our first and last creator
of all good things:
that breath of life
from atom to Adam;
from earth, to waters, to sky.
To see him ever-clearly.
To wonder at his living craft.
Every snowflake is unique.
Every soul, the only one
in infinitude.
And every bloom—
its pretty head—
given up for multitudes.
This is what he does.

And then,
like Christ—
His son—
and all those miracles.
Every broken thing healed.
Every bleeding woman touched.
Every motley soul invited to the banquet table.
And then,
every thief on a cross forgiven,
every shattered sinner saved,
every dead thing, at last, a resurrection song.
His very life, given up for the multitudes.
Yes, this is what he did.

So, as I strike this humble pen to page
in search of the clearest truth,
the most startling beauty. . .
the deepest secrets there are to say. . .
I am always drawn outward and upward,
unraveling lines and stanzas—
like a small expansion,
now a holy act,
to land on the mysteries of God:
to learn to know them. . .
to learn to name them. . .
And, then at last,
to breathe in awe of *Him*.

Wings

How precious is Your lovingkindness, O God!
Therefore the children of men
put their trust under the shadow of Your wings.

—Psalm 36:7

But those who wait on the LORD shall renew their strength;
They shall mount up with wings like eagles.
They shall run and not be weary.
They shall walk and not faint.

—Isaiah 40:31

MAN OF SORROWS

I will go to the woods
to write my poems to God
when the world is too much with me:
to drop on my knees,
to sing of my grief
and brokenness, hollowed out—
to say the words
they will not hear because
they cannot stand to know it—
to speak my sorrows,
to bear witness to my wounds,
to look and know
that suffering comes for us all.

Then, past the tree line I will go,
to the hill that is higher than me.
When man's compassion fails to know,
I will go to Calvary:
to lay my head at His feet—
to feel the damp earth on my face
and touch the dirt as the world grows dim—
to know the Man of Sorrows
and be known by the only one

who can hold the whole world in his hands
and my broken soul.

THIS HOLY BREAKING

I.

If there were ruined things,
it was You.
If the night was dark,
it was You.
And when the pain was too much,
it was You—

You and Your mysterious knowing,
You in the practice of breaking.

II.

Like Job—like testing—
You stripped him, like me,
of everything
because You knew
about his righteousness.
You offered him up
because You knew he loved
the Giver
and not His given things
more.

Like Jacob—a wrestling—
You touched his hip, like me,
to make him limp.
To give him
a new name
and to say,
My child, you struggled
with man and God
and have overcome.

III.

It was His steady hand,
this brutal love,
that birthed the stars
and shaped the seas.

And it was His mercy
in this holy breaking
that saved a wretch
like me.

ENTERTAINING ANGELS

after Hebrews 13:2

Late at night,
when I can't sleep
and my mind goes round and round,
I think I hear the pitter-patter of feet
outside my window.

It comes at 3:00 a.m.—
without fail—
and I imagine
it's an angel in my garden,
coming to visit our Mother Mary—
that majestic stone edifice
nestled among the pittosporum,
who prays over us,
day and night,
in her permanent refrain.

And all I can think of,
while I lie there in the dark,
is how much I *need* this to be true
and how much I hurt,
and how much I want

to walk out my door
into the warm night—
away from what haunts me—
with my bare feet in the damp grass
and invite her to come in for tea—
some chamomile and honey,
or whatever it is she pleases.

And while we wait for the bags to steep,
we'll sit at my kitchenette,
and I will ask her all of the questions
I have about Heaven
and God,
and what He's like up close,
and what it's like up there in the sky
where nothing hurts anymore—
where I'll finally see the babies I never held
and my grandmother—
young and cancer-free.
I'll tell her I have her lion's heart, after all,
and how beautiful she was in her wraps
when her hair fell out
and how sorry I am that I wasn't there to say goodbye—
even if I was just a child.

And then I'd want to know my guest.
So, I guess I'd ask her what it's like to have wings
and to exist and never ache like we humans do
at the end of things,
and how she found my garden bed,
and what brought her here:

Was it me?
Or my daughter sleeping
in the other room?
Or my husband who
is so very tired
after the many winters
we've endured?

I imagine we will be so engaged,
talking back and forth,
that I might forget about the tea—
steeping just a reach away.
But I'm sure she'd gently remind me—
like any good angel would.
I'd apologize, embarrassed,
and offer her some jam and toast.

Then we'd talk some more,
as we eat and drink,
deep beyond the din of night—
until at once we'd realize the sun,
waking up the world, again.

And then, I'd notice,
in an epiphany of sorts,
(as the light pours in
the east window,
proclaiming a new hope)
that our tea and toast
had become a breakfast—
and I was entertaining
angels unaware.

STILL LIFE

It is an ancient scene before me:

    a wooden table for banqueting
        (a rugged cross for crucifying,)

    with fruit ripened and cradled in baskets
        (a heart of flesh cupped by sagging ribs,)

    and roses in full bloom strewn about,
        (His head wilting in anguish beneath a crown,)

    a collection of life—
        (a sacrifice of life)

    with fine strings, prose, and ink wells.
        (with lashings, thorns, and driven nails.)

The perfect still life—yet amidst it all:

    a skull with black sockets—
    moribund yet hungry.
        (a divine mouth in grimace—
        wine-soaked yet thirsting.)

Giving warning:
    (Speaking love:)

Memento mori.
Or "Remember you must die."
    (*Hodie mecum eris en Paradiso.*
    or "Today you shall be with me in Paradise.")

Oh, it is the way of man—
that on our last day we go down to the dead!
    (Oh, it is the way of Christ—
    that on the third day he rose again!)

The End.
    (Selah and Amen.)

SPEECHLESS

I have thought so long,
but I cannot find
a fresh metaphor
or the right words
to say (just so)
what You are
and what I am not.

Like how I fail
and how You do not:
You, like pylons driven
deep into the ground
to sure up the shore.
You, holding earth in place
not matter
the midnight storms,
the beating winds,
the rising tides,
setting me awash.

Or, how I am so small
and You are not:
You, like the infinite
water's reach

spanning across oceans—
You, baptizing its
granule forms—
to smooth edges
to make pressure
for new life—
birthing a pearl
of great worth.

It's all been said,
I know.
So, I haven't
the right words
for You.
You, who are *The Word*—
the beginning
and the end.
And how I am not.

Or how You are every word
thereafter:
life breathed,
plucked from our thoughts,
bowed down
and speechless
before You.

A LITURGY FOR SUFFERING

Liturgy is a noun.
But, oh,
it is so much more:
a religious body of rites,
a customary series of ideas,
a song of worship,
and the "work of the people."

Oh, yes, we are a people
of liturgy,
aren't we?
We toil. We rest.
We sow. We reap.
We mourn. We laugh.
We dance. We sing.
All a holy act.

Our lives are in union,
a soul in every season—
and everything all at once.
We fling up our chorus
to the sky
and pray it echoes back—
to know God

and that we may be seen
in our triumphs
and tragedies.

Oh, we sing,
and every song has its parts:
a bridge,
a chorus—
its ebb and overflow.
And though we may suffer,
we are never alone
in our woeful verse.

For the God of the universe
moves in and through us.
And humanity groans
on our behalf.
So, we will raise our song,
this "work of the people,"
beyond our brokenness—
for the dancing will come,
and when it does
we will be free—
most free indeed.
Selah.
Selah.

ON PSALM 84

Come!
Sit and sip the air in through those boisterous lungs of yours.
Then stay silent for a little while.
Go out, walk widely, and watch the birds
    as they follow their roads in the sky toward their homes at night.
The trees await the sparrows to cradle their nests and hoards—
    all provided for.
The earth rests in a gentle hum, warm from the day's sun
for the marsh rabbits to settle into.
Stand at the wood's edge and touch the coming shadows.
Then drink and listen to the air slow dance in the maple trees
    as the gray fox retraces her steps to her burrow,
    and the bluegill drops down into his muddy-water cave.
Go quietly and see how stars are sometimes tucked behind clouds—
    Orion's Belt draped in a resting constellation
    or Aquarius in repose.
Even the sun goes to sleep in the horizon's crest,
    as the moon awakes from Heaven's meadow to sing its lullaby.
Oh, how there is shelter for everyone!
And for every shelter there is a soul in want!
And we too, the watchers, are in search of rest—
    a place where we can retrace our steps back to the beginning:
    a dwelling or a tabernacle.
Lord, either one will do!

THE ARRIVAL

I want to find the way back, and when I arrive,
   I want to carve out a space, in peace,
     and fill it with all the lovely things I never knew.
       It is said Eden will be at its center—
         walled off from the world
           by a circle of towering bushes.
             I will parachute in, and I will stay there,
               planting white gardenias
                 and pink saucer magnolias where I see fit,
                   adding to them all the time with heather
                   and wild zinnias of every shade.
                     It will be a place—so beautiful and in bloom–
                      where I am finally known
                       by the great Architect,
                       and I will find
                       no reason
                       to ever
                       leave.

EARTHBOUND

"God's people need to be carried. They are very heavy by nature. They have no wings, or if they have, they are like the dove of old that lay among the pots; and they need divine grace to make them rise up on wings covered with silver and with feathers of yellow gold. By nature, sparks fly upward, but the sinful souls of men fall downward."

—Charles Spurgeon

We are earthbound things:
heavy (and sometimes good) souls,
a diaspora cursed
to roam.

Sparks fly upward, yes,
and so do winged-things.
But surely never us.
No, we are tied downward.

They split the sky with wonder—
possessing fire and light.
Yet, ours is a destiny
made in bog and mire.

They are free, free, free—

the crane, the crow, the sparrow!
But they do not know
how free they are—I think.

Oh, we are the wingless made wild
only by our wondering,
possessing neither fire nor light
but only the faintest hope:

somewhere there is more,
and if we believe,
we will forever
be carried upward.

THAT WE MAY SEE ITS GOODNESS

after Proverbs 25:25

We are in the winter seasons now.
All stacked together—end to end.

And all we see through frosted windows
is falling snow on fallow ground.

There's news coming from the East,
saying that Spring has come to another town—

like folklore or myth from our old dusty books,
and we wonder what these Blooms might mean

and what a warm Sun could do, so we pray
with our mightiest petitions—all tears and calloused knees—

that this New Life will come here one day—
and that we may see its Goodness and be born once more:

like a green bud unfurling—
up from a Holy Ground.

I'D LIKE TO BELIEVE

I'd like to believe
that every key
my fingers press down
on my typewriter,
punches a hole in Heaven
among the low-hanging clouds
where I can hide my prayers—
there in parchment scrolls,
amid the dancing stars.

And I'd like to believe
that then the little angel,
who works the midnight shift
in Heaven's Basement
comes to gather all my songs
and hauls them up
the golden staircase
to sing my pleas to God.

THIS HOLY ACT

Something holy is afoot.

Do you feel it close, moving through the woods—
here within your reach?
Do you see how the soft pines glide through the frigid air—
still green with life—
and how the last copper leaf clings to the maple tree in the wind?
Or how the ivy crawls across the rock like an upward stream—
and how the chanterelle's yellow cup opens wide to be born at night?

Do you see how the stars seem to move and shake with verve
in the ancient sky and how they guide the deer and bear the same?
Or how the black atmosphere goes
on and on and on,
so hungry in the forever dance of creation beyond them—
ever expanding out into something new
and back to the starting touch of God,
when he breathed burning life into the dust
because of love
and birthed light?

In the beginning, it says,
God made the Heavens and the Earth.

Can you feel backward and trace it all to you?
Love begets love begets creation begets life begets love and so on:
from land, to sky, to lark, to wings,
to river, to trout, to mountains, to springs,
to face, to heart, to lips, to words.
All love.
All one,
beating in the same accord.
All happening *now*—
in soul and song.
All light, all good, all divine.

Yes, something holy is afoot.
Even now, as we doubt, or cry, or walk about, or bask in joy.
Even now, as we are born or born again,
are gaining or losing, are growing old or dying.
Even now, as we are opening our eyes to live or wake,
or are closing our eyes to pray or sleep a bit—
in heaven or in our dreams.

His kingdom come,
His will be done, it says,
on Earth as it is in Heaven.

It is all happening—all at once.
So, gasp *now*.
Hold your hand to your heart.
Know your own soul.
Then, stand back and see *anew*—
in this Holy Act.

THERE IS A DOOR

There is a road
that goes out
at night
into the dark
inside us all.

I have walked that road,
alone and broken,
in midnight hours,
in early morning hours
before the sun's come up,
before the world hums with life,
looking for a light,
spilling across the lawn
onto my path
from a cracked door,
unlocked and waiting
for me to follow
up over the sidewalk
onto the grassy knoll,
and into the entryway—
to knock,
to push through,
to see

that Love,
who is waiting
in the quiet,
whispering,
"*My child, My child.*"

OF WINGS AND DIRT

Oh, I have known dirt and flesh—
what it is to be broken in human form:
to be weighed down by sin and love,
to be overcome with beauty and devasting awe,
to squander youth and drink from infinitude,
and to hunger and starve and want too much
from everything I taste and touch.

And yet—
I have known wings, too,
and brushed against such lofty things:
to dream, pray, and eat the Good Word,
to taste Heaven and hear its hymns
sung in holy chorus inside my chest at 2:00 am
after I've cursed myself—
cursed it *all* again—
and drank my dram of sacred doubt
when darkness was my closest friend.

And I still hear the singing
of Sunday morning saints in steeples
and rise to their calling—
to feel the wooden pews against my spine,
to bow my head and nod *yes, yes,*

and yet find it hard to believe—
deep within me—
that *Hallelujah* song
of *healing*.

Yes, I know how to stand
and dance in my mind
so close to grace and white-hot peace
and yet never feel a thing
but the dirt beneath my feet
and the beating heart of Earth.

A divided body.
A bloodied saint.
I am holy, yet profane.
I believe, and then I doubt.
I am lost, yet I am found.

I am both—
of wings and dirt.
But still, Your blood says,
I am Yours.

Behold, I will do a new thing,
Now it shall spring forth;
Shall you not know it?
I will even make a road in the wilderness
And rivers in the desert.

—Isaiah 43:19

www.ingramcontent.com/pod-product-compliance
Lightning Source LLC
Chambersburg PA
CBHW062222080426
42734CB00010B/1987